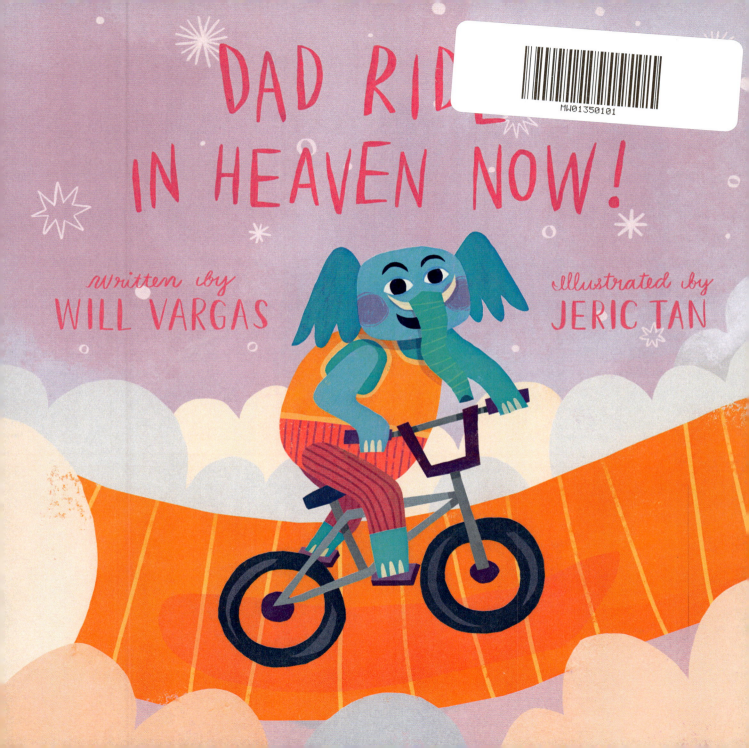

# DAD RIDES IN HEAVEN NOW!

Copyright © 2022 By The Anador Studio

This book was designed by The Anador Studio, written by Will Vargas, and illustrated by Jeric Tan.

The Anador Studios supports copyright. Copyright fuels creativity, encourages diverse voices, promotes free speech, and creates a vibrant culture. Thank you for buying an authorized edition of this book and complying with copyright laws by not reproducing, scanning, or distributing any part of it in any form without permission.

Ten percent of the book's proceeds will be given to Speed The Light, a student-initiated, volunteer, charitable program that provides much-needed equipment to missionaries across the nation and in over 180 countries around the world.

For more information about Speed the Light, visit www.Speedthelight.com.

Our books are based on real-life experiences by the Author.

For Information contact:

Wilfredo "Will" Vargas at vargasw@faithassembly.org

ISBN: 978-0-578-38471-9 (Paperback)
Library of Congress Cataloging-in-Publication Data is Available
Printed in the United States of America
10 9 8 7 6 5 4 3 2 1
First Edition: March 2022

Sometimes life makes us happy. Sometimes it makes us feel sad. In this little story, we meet William, an elephant who lost his dad!

He sat on his bed, missing him a lot. He was quiet, still, and feeling distraught. His mind was all foggy. He asked, "How can this be? How could my daddy leave me like this?"

Now in the playground, swinging alone, William had no one to push him along.

He saw Mr. Fox, and he saw Mr. Rabbit, but now no one like Dad is on this planet.

Missing him dearly, he swung back and forth. William felt lonely and terribly lost.

He asked the heavens, "God send me some peace, a part of my heart has lost a great piece."

William thought to himself,
Jumping, exploring, and video games, my dad always knew lots of silly games. I wonder and ponder if he thinks of me—there isn't a moment I don't think of him.

I know he is in heaven, God made it clear. I wish I had him to hug. I wish I had him near.

A warm cuddle from Mom made William feel safe while steady tears fell from their faces.

They wondered together if life would get better, but neither would know that they'd get stronger together!

William's dad was cool and extreme! He played with his bike day out and day in!

Dad thought to himself,

Jumping, exploring, and video games, with my dear William I played silly games. I wonder and ponder if he thinks of me. There isn't a moment I don't think of him.

I know he is on Earth, God made it clear. I wish I had him to hug. I wish I had him near.

Now in heaven riding alone, Dad had no one to cheer him along.

Looking down, he saw Mr. Fox, and he saw
Mr. Rabbit, but for William there was now no one like Dad on his planet.

Missing him dearly, he rode back and forth. Dad felt lonely and terribly lost.

He asked the heavens, "God send me some peace, a part of my heart has lost a great piece."

Stomp! Stomp! Baby William was growing!

Stomp! Stomp! Baby William has grown!

Life has been different.

Life has been hard, but I know dad has seen me grow from afar!

*In loving memory of*
**Christopher Vargas**

Son, brother, fantastic father, loyal friend & BMX fanatic!

## ABOUT THE AUTHOR

Will Vargas has always been creative and desires to "make things pretty." As a kid, he always played teacher or sketched anything that came to mind. After losing his youngest brother, Will found himself in a difficult place when his nephew, who had just lost his dad, started asking questions he did not have the answers to. Since then, he has become passionate about finding ways to connect with his nephews and nieces as they grow and learn to process their emotions. He discovered that he could communicate effectively with them through art, thus creating his first book, *Dad Rides In Heaven Now!*. He is also working on other stories to help kids deal with other challenging issues affecting their lives and emotions.

Will is the Design Lead at Faith Assembly. On the weekends, you can find him drinking chocolate milk and eating glazed donuts. Will lives in Florida with his two hermit crabs, Fred and George.

### HI!
I'M WILL! THANK YOU FOR LETTING ME INTO YOUR KIDS LIBRARY!

### Acknowledgments

To God for making this happen.
To Noah for inspiring me to write to kids.
To my family for being so supportive.
To Jeric, who made all this come true with his talents.
To Kathy for giving me, William!
And Chris, who I miss dearly.

Love you guys!

## ABOUT THIS BOOK

*Dad Rides in Heaven Now!* is a story that helps kids of all ages understand the emotions that may arise when a family is navigating through grief. Grief can be a heavy topic to explain, and often kids come with many questions and big emotions that need to be processed. *Dad Rides in Heaven Now!* portrays the unfortunate loss of a son, brother, and father and a family's attempt to bring healing to their broken hearts. It symbolizes grief processed and memories kept for later reading. We hope this story tells your kids that they are still loved and not forgotten by those who are no longer with us.

Follow us on Instagram @theanadorstudio

Made in United States
North Haven, CT
16 September 2023